REAL MEN ARE
GODLY

John Greening

Regular Baptist Press
Building Lives by the Book
www.RegularBaptistPress.org

Real Men Are Godly
© 2001 • Regular Baptist Press • Schaumburg, Illinois
www.RegularBaptistPress.org • 1-800-727-4440
All rights reserved • Printed in U.S.A.
RBP5253 • ISBN: 978-0-87227-211-8

Sixth printing—2014

Contents

Preface

Paying taxes, meeting deadlines, commuting to work, dealing with coworkers, being congenial to neighbors, waiting in line at the store, getting along as a family, keeping the car operating, or planning income for retirement—do these activities sound familiar to you? Life is full of pressing demands. Do you approach all of life in a godly manner?

You may think that the character of godliness belongs only to pastors who make their living doing church, to people who have time on their hands, or to women who seem to be naturally spiritual. The truth is, godliness is not for a select few. Godly living is a possibility for every follower of Christ, including real men.

In this study you will investigate Job, a man who integrated godliness into the entire scope of his life. You will discover that Job's life was more than suffering and sorrow. He was a real man who faced the same challenges as you. What set Job apart was his determination to do everything in a godly manner. As you study these lessons on your own or with a group of men, you will learn how godliness can become part of every area of your life. ***Real*** men are **godly!**

A Real Man

This study will help you view every dimension of your life as an opportunity to exhibit godliness.

You've probably come across a T-shirt with the expression "Real Men . . ." The idea is that if a man is truly a man, he will evidence his masculinity by entering into certain activities. The following expressions are some slightly slanted samples.

- Real men drink their coffee straight.
- Real men don't go shopping.
- Real men are on the green in two on a par five.
- Real men don't use instruction manuals.
- Real men show off their injuries.
- Real men have a refrigerator on the front porch, a car on blocks in the yard, and old tires on the roof.

And my favorite—

- Real men need only three things to be successful: duct tape, WD-40, and a good dog.

Real Godliness

If you are a real man who is a Christian, your life is to evidence a most important attribute, that of godly character.

1. In your circle of acquaintances, what man stands out as being godly? What about him causes you to view him in that manner?

What activities characterize real godly men? We often assess a man's godliness by measuring his involvement in three major activities:

- daily devotions (Bible reading and prayer);
- church involvement (attendance and service);
- witnessing.

We think that if a man meets these three essential standards, then certainly he must be godly! Undoubtedly these activities are vitally important. However, in themselves they are not the sum total of godliness. Many more components fill a man's average day.

2. List some of the responsibilities that you have in your life.

Godliness is intended to be a pervasive quality that penetrates every dimension of a man's life—his work ethic, money management, treatment of people, commitment to his family, and much more. To be godly is to conduct oneself in a truly Godlike manner.

3. What unique design feature did God give to man (Genesis 1:27)?

Man was created to reflect the character and glory of God. But like a deadly disease, sin infected man.

4. What profile of man do you find in Romans 3:10–18?

5. How does man match up to the character of God (Romans 3:23)?

Because of sin, God's original design for man was distorted and hidden, just as if mud were thrown on a great work of art. But through the salvation that God offers, restoration can begin.

6. What is the ultimate purpose of the salvation that God extends (Romans 8:29)?

Man can again be conformed to the character of God.

7. How does one take advantage of this salvation (Romans 10:9, 13)?

Godliness can be a part of a man's life. God desires that godliness (His character) be integrated into all areas of life, not compartmentalized in a few.

8. How did Paul describe total-life godliness in 1 Corinthians 10:31?

Paul provided a similar challenge in Colossians 3:17: "And whatsoever ye do in word or deed, do all in the name of the Lord Jesus."

9. Into what areas of life should you integrate godliness according to the following verses in Colossians?
   3:18, 19

   3:20, 21

   3:22—4:1

   4:2–4

   4:5

   4:6

An Excellent Example

Since godliness may seem like an abstract concept, its meaning becomes clearer when we observe a real-life example. Though the Bible contains many godly role models, one outstanding example is Job.

The distinguishing mark of Job is often his suffering. While enduring suffering is an outstanding trait of Job, many other positive attributes characterize this godly man.

10. How does Job 1:1 describe Job?

11. Job had many responsibilities. What areas of his life do you find in Job 1:2–5 and 29:12–17 and 21–23?

As a husband, father, neighbor, businessman, and citizen, Job conducted himself in a manner that matched the character of God. Godliness for Job was not compartmentalized in a confined segment of his life, nor was it reduced to a religious ritual. Godliness evidenced itself in everything Job did.

Job was not a pastor or clergyman. Sometimes we place those individuals in a special category and assume a separate standard exists for other men. Job claimed no separate standard.

Job was a man with a demanding job and a large family. He lived as an active participant in his community. He was a man with enormous responsibilities and a busy schedule.

12. Write a description of the areas of Job's life listed on page 12.

Family (Job 1:2, 4)

Business (Job 1:3)

Religious (Job 1:5)

Political (Job 29:7–11)

Community service (Job 29:12–17)

Job's distinction came not from his large family, business success, or fame, but because his life reflected the character of God in everything he did.

This study is designed to assist you in the ongoing adventure of integrating godliness into every dimension of your life. The process of pursuing godliness requires effort, but the results are worth the investment.

A Real-Life Model

Do you evidence godliness in every dimension of your life? Could you honestly wear a T-shirt that said . . .

Real men love their wives.

Real men give attention to their families.

Real men treat everyone with respect.

Real men work hard.

Real men use self-control.

Real men remain faithful to God no matter what happens.

Take a few moments and consider the Life Areas listed on the chart on page 13. Think about your success (or lack of success) in integrating godliness into each area. Then rate your **GQ** (godliness quotient) according to the extent of your godly living.

Godliness Quotient Chart

Put a checkmark in the column that best describes your godliness in each life area.

Life Areas	Mastered	Taking Positive Steps Forward	Mediocre	Below Average	Needing Major Work
Marriage					
Family					
Job performance					
Work colleagues					
Church					
Hobbies					
Finances					
Friendships					
Vacation					
Community service					
Education					
Fitness					
Neighbors					
Chores					
Extended family					

The apostle Peter was a man who accepted the responsibility and challenge of integrating godliness into every area of his life.

13. What reassuring promise did Peter share (2 Peter 1:3)?

14. What did Peter say about the process of developing godliness (2 Peter 1:5–8)?

The road to godliness begins with a first step. You must trust Jesus Christ as your Savior. Godliness is not the achievement of a lifetime of self-effort, but it is the product of a life transformed by God's grace. Place your faith in Christ, and you will be saved. "For God so loved the world, that he gave his only begotten Son, that whosoever believeth in him should not perish, but have everlasting life" (John 3:16).

Once you trust Christ as your Savior, godliness is within your grasp. The resources to assist you in developing the character of God are freely available. The challenge is for you to begin moving toward that goal. The benefits of godliness are worth the effort: "Godliness is profitable unto all things, having promise of the life that now is, and of that which is to come" (1 Timothy 4:8).

A Verse to Memorize

"According as his divine power hath given unto us all things that pertain unto life and godliness, through the knowledge of him that hath called us to glory and virtue" (2 Peter 1:3).

A Respected Man

This study will prompt you to evaluate your reputation in the eyes of your acquaintances and God.

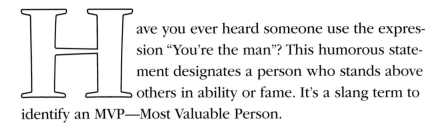ave you ever heard someone use the expression "You're the man"? This humorous statement designates a person who stands above others in ability or fame. It's a slang term to identify an MVP—Most Valuable Person.

Respected by God

If God were selecting someone on whom to bestow the MVP distinction, He might have said, "Job, you're the man!"

1. How did God describe Job in Job 1:8?

Can you imagine having such a reputation that God Himself would describe you as the No. 1 godly man above all others? That is quite a distinction!

2. If God described your reputation, what might He say?

You might conclude from God's description that Job was sinless. That was not the case.

3. How do you know from Romans 5:12 that Job was a sinner?

Since Job was a sinner, what did God mean when He referred to him as "perfect" and "upright"? The use of the word "perfect" does not imply sinless perfection. Rather, it suggests that Job was mature, complete, or whole. We might say that he had it all together.

Job was also "upright." This word implies the idea of being morally straight.

4. With what lifestyles are the words "straight" or "not straight" associated today?

According to God, Job was morally and ethically straight as an arrow. He hit the mark.

It was also said of Job, "He feareth God."

5. What do you think it means to fear God?

I had a healthy fear of my dad. He was not harsh or unkind. Actually, he was very loving. However, I knew that he was the head of our family. His words and role carried authority. I loved him and held him in high regard. I knew that he expected me to do what he said. His rules were not to be broken. If I disobeyed, I faced the consequences.

Job had a high level of love and respect for God. He did not take His authority lightly. When God said something, Job knew He meant it.

6. What evidence of respect do you hear in Job's words directed to God in Job 42:1–6?

We are also told that Job shunned evil.

7. What is the meaning of the word "shunned"?

When Job shunned evil, he wanted no part of any activities that were morally unacceptable to God.

The act of shunning may be illustrated by your typical response to telemarketing calls that come during dinner. You probably make it clear to the sales representative that you don't want to be bothered. You quickly cut off the call. In a sense you are "shunning" the caller. In a similar manner, you should promptly disconnect from any solicitations to evil.

Job shunned evil because he feared God. He took God's reality, authority, and holiness seriously. Job made himself accountable to God. He wanted no part of sin.

8. What do Proverbs 8:13 and 16:6 say is the outcome of fearing God?

Job didn't live in an evil-free or problem-free environment. The placement of the book of Job in Scripture is immediately prior to Psalms, but Bible scholars suggest that Job may actually have been a contemporary of Abraham.

9. If Job lived in the time period of Abraham, what evil influences might have been present in a well-known city of ill-repute (Genesis 13:12, 13; 19:4–9)?

Job lived in a culture where evil was present, but he shunned it. He remained morally straight, or upright. He had his life together. Job was a man of integrity despite the pressures and temptations that surrounded him.

10. Think of an area in which you are tempted by evil. List the steps that you might take to shun evil.

    Area of temptation _____

    Steps to shun evil

    •

    •

    •

Respected by Men

Not only did God respect Job, but his neighbors and countrymen respected him also.

11. What evidence do you find in Job 29:7–12 and 21–25 that Job was highly respected in his community?

Those who knew Job held him in high regard as a man of character and wisdom.

12. How do Proverbs 22:1 and Ecclesiastes 7:1 describe the value of a good reputation?

13. What comes to mind when you observe the following Bible characters' reputations?

    Moses (Numbers 12:3)

David (Acts 13:22)

Judas (John 12:3–6)

Demas (2 Timothy 4:10)

Diotrephes (3 John 9, 10)

14. What areas do you need to strengthen to establish a good reputation?

Solomon shared an object lesson in Ecclesiastes 10:1 of two flies that were attracted to a jar of expensive perfume. Enticed by the fragrance, they soon found themselves trapped in the sticky perfume gel. After an intense struggle to free themselves, they succumbed. The heat of the day gradually caused their carcasses to decay. It was not long before the once appealing fragrance became a repulsive smell. Solomon used this illustration to underscore the importance of not permitting the enticement of sin to lure us into actions that will destroy our reputation. "Dead flies cause the ointment of the apothecary to send forth a stinking savour: so doth a little folly him that is in reputation for wisdom and honour" (Ecclesiastes 10:1). Don't allow your life to develop a foul reputation. It's better to be known as a godly man.

A Verse to Memorize

> *"A good name is better than precious ointment"* (Ecclesiastes 7:1).

A Falsely Accused Man

This study will encourage you to act godly under pressure.

Chicago newspapers and television stations carried a story about Anthony Porter—a man wrongfully accused of murder who lived for eighteen years on death row. A professor and group of students from Northwestern University began to examine his case. Convinced that Porter had been improperly charged, they painstakingly reassembled the evidence. Ultimately they were able to prove that Anthony Porter could not be guilty. Within weeks of his scheduled execution, Anthony Porter was released from jail, walking away as a free man.

Can you imagine the frustration, anger, and eventual despair of being declared guilty of a crime but of knowing you were innocent? Those who originally respected you had turned their backs on you. Even your friends assumed you were guilty.

Unjustly Criticized

Job was on the receiving end of serious accusations. An initial charge by a harsh critic led to a series of devastating tragedies. Those in Job's circle of acquaintances assumed that he was involved in some hidden evil. They were ignorant of what was actually going on behind the scenes. Popular opinion overruled the truth, and Job became a marked man.

1. Who initially accused Job (Job 1:6–9)?

2. How is Job's accuser described (Job 1:7; 1 Peter 5:8)?

3. What was it about Job that irritated Satan (Job 1:9)?

4. How do you think Satan reacts when you live a godly life?

5. What accusation did Satan make to God against Job (Job 1:9, 10)?

6. What did Satan propose as a way to prove Job's guilt (Job 1:11)?

Satan was attempting to get Job to crack under pressure. He believed that Job's godliness was due to the good times he was experiencing. Satan assumed that if the blessings were withdrawn, then the real Job would be exposed.

7. Why do you think some people might buckle under Satan's proposed plan?

8. How did God respond to Satan's proposal (Job 1:12)?

At first glance, God might appear to be weak by giving in to Satan. In reality, God was making a point to Satan by agreeing to the test. God wanted Satan to know that He, God, is the ultimate authority. Satan could do only what God allowed. God also wanted to underscore the nature of true godliness through His servant Job. True godliness remains consistent even under intense pressure. It submits to God's authority.

9. List the tragedies that happened to Job, as recorded in Job chapter 1.
   verses 13–15

   verse 16

   verse 17

   verses 18, 19

10. How did Job respond to this crushing series of events (Job 1:20–22)?

11. Did Job's response to the test stop Satan from looking for trouble (Job 2:1–3)?

12. How did God describe the consistency of Job's character (Job 2:3)?

13. What further challenge did Satan present to God (Job 2:4, 5)?

14. What did God permit Satan to do to Job (Job 2:6–8)?

15. What suggestion did Job's wife give to Job in regard to responding to his physical ailments (Job 2:9)?

16. How did Job respond to his wife and to this trial (Job 2:10)?

Real godliness consistently endures under the harshest of accusations and the most intense suffering.

More Critics

An additional source of accusations surfaced against Job. This time his friends, who initially comforted him (Job 2:11–13), turned on him.

17. What conclusions did each of Job's friends draw about Job's character?

Eliphaz (Job 4:7–11)

Bildad (Job 18:5–7)

Zophar (Job 20:1–29)

18. What effect did Job's circumstances and critics have on his reputation among his countrymen (Job 30:1–15)?

19. What do you learn from Jesus about godliness under false accusations?
Matthew 5:11, 12

Matthew 5:43–48

Matthew 10:16–26

Luke 23:34

Conducting yourself in a godly manner in the face of criticism and false accusations is not easy. It requires great reliance upon God's strength and a discipline to not react in a harsh manner. God will help you to exhibit His character even under intense pressure.

20. What illustration of false accusations did Peter give (1 Peter 2:18–20)?

21. What example of proper conduct did Peter share (1 Peter 2:21–23)?

22. What lessons do you learn from this model of godliness?

Godliness is not for cowards. Living out God's character in a hostile environment takes courage and determination. Jesus demonstrated this kind of courage and determination. Hebrews 12:1 and 2 challenge us, "Let us lay aside every weight, and the sin which doth so easily beset us, and let us run with patience the race that is set before us, looking unto Jesus the author and finisher of our faith; who for the joy that was set before him endured the cross, despising the shame, and is set down at the right hand of the throne of God." Real men live like Jesus!

A Verse to Memorize

"For this is thankworthy, if a man for conscience toward God endure grief, suffering wrongfully" *(1 Peter 2:19).*

A Confident Man

This study will help you realize that God fully equips you for godly living.

I magine this scenario: You are summoned to appear before a powerful judge and a jury of your peers. Your accuser has charged you with the crime of posing as a godly man. What evidence would you assemble to prove beyond reasonable doubt that your godliness is genuine? How would you argue in your own defense?

List the evidence you would present.

Would you be willing to swear to the truthfulness of that evidence by making the following statement: If I have not been honest and accurate in the presentation of this evidence, then may a car hit and kill me when I leave the courthouse? Job confidently made a similar statement when he was called before a judge and jury to defend the genuineness of his godliness.

Godliness on Trial

Job was an extraordinary man. Consider his profile (Job 1:1–8):

- a successful businessman with a significant portfolio of assets and a large workforce;
- a committed family man;
- a highly respected and influential community leader;
- a godly man with God's glowing endorsement.

Job seemed to have everything going for him. Suddenly the events in his life took a negative turn. With no warning or explanation, a series of tragedies stripped everything from him. His family, property, possessions, reputation, and health vaporized unexpectedly.

Perplexed and reeling from his experiences, Job laid out a defense of his own righteous character. Unaware of the discussion that had taken place between Satan and God and the subsequent tests that Satan administered, Job passionately argued his case. He was defending himself not only to a jury of his peers but also before the Judge of the universe, God.

Job 29—31 contains a summary of Job's arguments.

1. In chapter 29 Job rehearsed his past as a man of righteous character held in high esteem. Read this chapter and summarize the content.

2. In chapter 30 Job described who he had become—a broken man, despised by former friends and acquaintances. Read this chapter and summarize the content.

In chapter 31 Job illustrated who he was as a person. By means of eleven examples from his own life, he presented the evidence of his righteous conduct. Job was not boasting; he was honestly and humbly making his case. He declared himself to be a godly man who did not deserve to be punished for evil he had never done. So confident was Job of his defense that he was willing to accept specific consequences if he was not telling the truth. Job's eleven-point defense provides a wonderful picture of a man who took a total-life approach to godliness.

3. Develop an outline of Job's defense in Job 31 by filling in the chart on page 32. (This exercise will introduce you to chapter 31. We will investigate this chapter's contents in subsequent lessons.)

Job's Eleven-Point Defense

Read the following verses and record Job's godly action.

Job 31	Job's Godly Action (the evidence of his righteous conduct)	Job's Supporting Arguments
#1 (vv. 1–4)	Did not look upon a woman	God sees all
#2 (vv. 5–8)		God knows all and evaluates
#3 (vv. 9–12)		Judgment and destruction follow unfaithfulness
#4 (vv. 13–15)		Origin recognizes equality
#5 (vv. 16–23)		Examples of care
#6 (vv. 24, 25)		Rejected temporal security
#7 (vv. 26–28)		Refused false worship
#8 (vv. 29, 30)		Did not wish evil on enemies
#9 (vv. 31, 32)		An open home
#10 (vv. 33, 34)		An open life
#11 (vv. 38–40)		Cared for land and met obligations

Four important big-picture observations underscore the content of Job 31.

- Job's defense was not an arrogant expression of self-promotion, but was a confident self-appraisal of a godly man.
- Job had God on his defense team, even though Job didn't realize God's intentions. God was not like a prosecutor who was building a case against Job (vv. 35–37). Read again God's words in Job 1:8 and 2:3.
- Job integrated godliness into every dimension of his life. He did not take a compartmentalized approach to living out the character of God in only certain areas.
- Job had a sophisticated understanding of morality and ethics. No written revelation from God existed at that time. Job's morality and ethics came from a heart and conscience that were in tune with the Lord.

These observations have implications for you. When you live out the character of God, you will develop confidence. Your confidence will not be in yourself, but in the Lord. Instead of exalting yourself, you will glorify the Lord. When you obediently follow God's Word, you can be confident though the whole world may be against you.

4. Summarize these verses in your own words.

1 Peter 2:12

1 Peter 2:15

1 Peter 2:19

If you have trusted Jesus Christ as your Savior, then be assured that God is on your defense team. You are secure in God's salvation.

5. What assurance of God's commitment to you do you find in Romans 8:31–39?

God intends that His character be integrated into every area of your life.

6. Review the Godliness Quotient chart in lesson 1 (p. 13). How does your godliness in the areas listed compare to Job's total-life approach to godliness? Identify your strengths and weaknesses in godly living.

Godly Living	
Strengths	**Weaknesses**

You possess the completed Bible and an empowering salvation. Job was able to live a godly life as an Old Testament saint without these benefits. You have everything you need to be a godly man.

7. How does 2 Corinthians 9:8 emphasize this truth?

Confident godliness does not rest on one's own abilities or righteousness but on the abilities and righteousness of Christ. As you grow in your understanding of the grace of God, you will discover that He equips you with all of the resources you need to live out His character. Your responsibility is to rise to the challenge and do what God has equipped you to do—be a godly man.

A Verse to Memorize

> *"And God is able to make all grace abound toward you; that ye, always having all sufficiency in all things, may abound to every good work" (2 Corinthians 9:8).*

A Genuine Man

*This study will motivate you
to practice integrity in every
area of your life.*

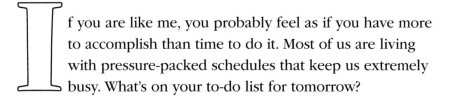

I f you are like me, you probably feel as if you have more
to accomplish than time to do it. Most of us are living
with pressure-packed schedules that keep us extremely
busy. What's on your to-do list for tomorrow?

1. Fill in the following planning chart of your anticipated
   schedule for tomorrow.
   6:00 A.M.

   7:00 A.M.

   8:00 A.M.

   9:00 A.M.

   10:00 A.M.

   11:00 a.m.

12:00 P.M.

1:00 P.M.

2:00 P.M.

3:00 P.M.

4:00 P.M.

5:00 P.M.

6:00 P.M.

7:00 P.M.

8:00 P.M.

9:00 P.M.

10:00 P.M.

When thinking about completing the items on your to-do list, do you also think about the manner in which you will do those tasks?

2. Look back through the list. How will godliness evidence itself in each of your anticipated activities?

Job was a busy man. He had a large ranch, a demanding job, a big family, and a full agenda of community responsibilities.

Job's to-do list was probably filled with more duties than two men could handle.

When Job began each day, he put on godliness in a manner similar to slipping on his clothes. From the start to the finish of every day, Job approached his responsibilities with this question in mind: How does God want me to live? Job was truly a man who had it all together.

3. How would you define integrity?

4. From recent news stories, provide an illustration of a person who exhibits integrity and an illustration of a person who lacks integrity.

Exhibits integrity—

Lacks integrity—

Job was a man of integrity. His public life matched his private life. He was not duplicitous. His internal thoughts matched his external actions. Consistency and authenticity marked him. Job evidenced integrity in three ways: by the disciplined use of his eyes, by his honesty, and by his marital faithfulness. As you study Job's life of integrity, ask yourself, "Does every part of my life reflect integrity?"

Evidence 1—Disciplined Eyes

5. What determination did Job make about his eyes (Job 31:1)?

Job's covenant does not suggest the inappropriateness of looking at a woman. Instead he is referring to refraining from a look that inspects and lingers, then permits the imagination to play out a lustful scenario.

6. How did King David violate this discipline (2 Samuel 11:2–4)?

7. What standard did Jesus establish for your eyes and thoughts (Matthew 5:27, 28)?

8. What consequences for disregarding this standard did Job mention (Job 31:2, 3)?

9. How are these consequences illustrated in the account of the undisciplined young man in Proverbs 7?

10. What ability of God, mentioned in Job 31:4, should act as a deterrent to undisciplined eyes?

How can a man develop disciplined eyes in an unrestrained culture? That is a great challenge. Your pastor will gladly and confidentially help you address this issue if you will ask for his counsel. Here are three basic principles that will help you to develop disciplined eyes.
- Learn to focus on Christ (Colossians 3:1–4).
- Learn to focus on your wife (Proverbs 5:14–20).
- Learn to focus on what is good (Philippians 4:8).

Evidence 2—Honesty

11. How is honesty important in the business practices of the following men?

    A pharmacist

    An auto mechanic

    A traveling salesman

    A lawyer

    A doctor

    A politician

12. What practices did Job avoid according to Job 31:5 and 6?

13. As a rancher and employer, how might Job have been tempted to be dishonest?

14. What evaluation was Job willing to undergo (Job 31:6)?

15. What consequences was Job willing to accept if he was found guilty of dishonesty (Job 31:7, 8)?

Evidence 3—Marital Faithfulness

16. What threat to godliness did Job avoid in Job 31:9?

17. What impact would compromise in this area have on Job (Job 31:11, 12)?

18. What relevant counsel did Solomon share (Proverbs 5:1–14; 6:20–29)?

19. How did Joseph avoid succumbing to this temptation (Genesis 39:1–12)?

20. What excuses might a man use in his attempt to rationalize marital unfaithfulness?

21. What principles of moral purity did Paul communicate in 1 Thessalonians 4:1–8?

Are you a man of integrity in the three areas mentioned in this study: disciplined eyes, honesty, and marital faithfulness (or, for the single man, moral purity)? Ask God to help you conduct a self-evaluation. If you have a problem, admit it. God already knows your problem, but you must acknowledge reality before you can take the necessary steps to change. King David had to first admit his sin; then he could begin the process of rebuilding his life. He exclaimed, "When I kept silence, my bones waxed old through my roaring all the day long. For day and night thy hand was heavy upon me: my moisture is turned into the drought of summer. Selah. I acknowledged my sin unto thee, and mine iniquity have I not hid. I said, I will confess my transgressions unto the LORD; and thou forgavest the iniquity of my sin. Selah" (Psalm 32:3–5). God is ready to forgive and restore you if you will be transparent in acknowledging your sin (1 John 1:9).

A Verse to Memorize

"Judge me, O LORD; for I have walked in mine integrity: I have trusted also in the LORD; therefore I shall not slide" (Psalm 26:1).

A Compassionate Man

This study will prompt you to consider the thoughts and needs of others.

Oxymorons are unusual expressions created by putting two contrasting words together. Here are a few examples: faulty logic, first deadline, clean dirt, intense apathy, civil war, freezer burn, political promise, extensive briefing, randomly organized, old news, fish farm, fairly stable, working vacation, a few more, or free agent.

Here's another expression some might view as an oxymoron—*compassionate man*. In our culture the thought surfaces that compassion fits better with women than it does with men. Males are portrayed as tough, decision-makers, action oriented, and unemotional. If men were to appear as anything less, they would risk being labeled feminine.

1. List some stereotypical activities—"men stuff"—that men do.

Anybody who carefully reads the book of Job would never question the masculinity of Job. He was a man's man. However, Job's masculinity did not exclude a compassionate dimension. A man will limit the influence of godliness in his life if he chooses to be insensitive toward others. Job's life is a challenge to every man to be considerate of the thoughts and needs of others around him.

Job evidenced his big heart in two ways—in his employee relationships and in his compassionate acts.

Employee Relationships

Job must have had a significant workforce to help him care for his ranch (Job 1:15–17). Creating a positive environment for his employees was not an easy task. Managing his workers was a major responsibility. Job held his staff in high regard. My hunch is that Job's employees appreciated their boss.

Not every boss is like Job.

2. Describe an insensitive boss you may have had.

3. How do you think an employer should respond to employee complaints or criticism?

4. Describe the positive management practice Job implied in Job 31:13.

Job asked two logical questions in Job 31:14. If he did not give attention to the feedback of his employees, how would he respond when God confronted him about his actions? Would Job also not listen to Him? It is easy to slip into the bad habit of not tuning in to criticism. We may assume we are always right, when in reality another person may see something we do not see. Proverbs 15:31 and 32 contain valuable counsel: "The ear that heareth the reproof of life abideth among the wise. He that refuseth instruction despiseth his own soul: but he that heareth reproof getteth understanding."

5. Job had an underlying view of employees that motivated him to react respectfully toward his workers' complaints (Job 31:15). What was it?

On an organizational chart, a boss appears above his employees. The role of a leader requires making tough decisions. His course of action may not always be popular with everybody, but he should always be open to employee feedback.

6. How could a boss encourage employee feedback?

7. What environment would an employer need to create for employees to feel free to express themselves?

8. What benefits come to a business or organization when employers and employees work together to find solutions to problems?

Compassionate Acts

Job was known for his kindness. Although he was an important man with a busy schedule, he humbly reached out to needy people.

9. What specific examples of his compassion did Job mention in the following verses?
   31:16

   31:17, 18

   31:19, 20

   31:21

10. What consequence did Job say he was willing to accept if he was not honestly portraying his compassion (Job 31:22)?

11. What lessons do you learn about caring for the needs of others from the following passages?
Proverbs 22:9, 16, 22, 23

Matthew 25:35–40

Luke 10:25–37

1 Timothy 5:3–10

James 1:27—2:9

1 John 3:16–18

12. List some individuals you know who could be classified in the following categories.
The poor

Widows

Fatherless

13. What could you do to assist the poor?

14. What could you do to assist widows?

15. What could you do to assist the fatherless?

16. What present-day examples do you know of individuals or groups helping people in need?

17. What could a group of men from your church do to help people in need?

I knew a man who was a boxer in his youth. His face still showed the signs of earlier battles. Long ago, he hung up his gloves. His exercise took a different form. Every Sunday morning he drove to an apartment complex occupied primarily by people on welfare. He picked up a small, wheelchair-bound man to bring him to church. It was a special sight to watch this rugged man gently lift a frail man who could do little on his own. Jesus often did such loving acts (e.g., Mark 1:29–31, 40–42; 6:37–42; 10:13–16). Real men are compassionate toward others.

A Verse to Memorize

> *"Finally, be ye all of one mind, having compassion one of another, love as brethren, be pitiful, be courteous" (1 Peter 3:8).*

A Values-Oriented Man

This study will help you recognize the need to develop Biblical guiding principles.

H is substance also was seven thousand sheep, and three thousand camels, and five hundred yoke of oxen, and five hundred she asses, and a very great household; so that this man was the greatest of all the men of the east" (Job 1:3). That's quite a ranch! Job was managing a big-time business. If he were living today, his name would probably appear on the list of wealthiest CEOs.

Whenever a man's responsibilities increase, life becomes more complicated. Many businesspeople find themselves under increasing ethical and moral pressure.

1. What dangers often accompany growing assets according to Jesus' teaching in Luke 12:13–21?

People can easily begin to covet, misplace priorities, and accumulate possessions to the neglect of their eternal destiny.

Consider these two successful businessmen. Both have accumulated considerable assets. They are prominent men in their communities. The first man has made the Lord a priority in his life. Prayer and Bible study are a disciplined part of his daily routine. The heavy demands of his work do not distract him from his service in church. He steadfastly refuses to compromise his integrity in business dealings. He treats his workers with respect. He has a strong relationship with his wife and children. His family is walking with the Lord. Believers and nonbelievers hold him in high regard.

The second man is a marginal Christian. His work is a constant distraction from his walk with the Lord. He is too busy to attend church and rarely gets involved. The temptations of the business world exert a constant pull on him. Questionable activities are present in some of his dealings. His family is in turmoil. He seems more interested in multiplying his investments than growing in his walk with the Lord.

2. Compare and contrast the lives of these two men. How do their priorities differ?

Job was a busy man with large commercial holdings. His success, coupled with his commitment to God, made him a high-profile target for Satan. Despite the great pressures that were on him, Job retained his loyalty to God.

Job's "core values" were one of the main reasons for the stability and strength of his relationship with God. Core values are guiding principles that are developed deep within a man. Like a high-tech navigational system, they direct him in making life's choices.

What guiding principles direct you? Consider two core values in Job's life: his source of security and his priority in worship. He found his security in the Lord rather than in temporal commodities, and he acknowledged the God of creation as the supreme ruler of his life.

Source of Security

3. What did Job *not* stake his life on according to Job 31:24 and 25?

Job found his security and identity in the Lord. That is why Job remained faithful to the Lord when everything was taken away from him.

4. How did Job view his possessions (Job 1:21)?

5. What threats regarding money did the apostle Paul address in 1 Timothy 6:9 and 10?

6. What important lesson did Paul teach in 1 Timothy 6:6–8?

7. What did Paul say a man *should* pursue (1 Timothy 6:11, 12)?

8. What investment plan is recommended in 1 Timothy 6:17–19?

9. What changes do you need to make with your material assets based on this study?

Priority of Worship

Job lived in a pagan culture. He was surrounded by people who worshiped animals, insects, birds, trees, rivers, the sun, the moon, and stars.

10. How did men develop a pagan mind-set (Romans 1:18–23)?

11. What are the inevitable consequences of a pagan mind-set (Romans 1:24–32)?

12. How did Job react to the pagan enticement of nature (Job 31:26–28)?

The word "enticed" in verse 27 is the same word translated "deceived" in verse 9. It refers to the enticement of sexual temptation. "My mouth hath kissed my hand" is an obscure expression, probably descriptive of throwing a kiss of affection—in this case toward these objects of worship.

13. In the following passages, what did God say about the worship of any other gods but Him?
Exodus 20:1–6

Psalm 115

Most of us would not recognize any personal connection to the pagan worship of nature. However, does the lure of the ocean, mountains, or streams entice us away at times from focusing our worship on God? I enjoy outdoor activities and fresh air. It is healthy to get outside and recreate. God made His creation for us to enjoy. We can even see His handiwork in His creation. Yet we must never become more enamored with the creation than with the Creator.

14. What object lessons from His creation did God use to teach Job (Job 38—41)? List as many examples as you find.

15. How did Job respond to God's lessons from creation (Job 40:3–5; 42:1–3)?

16. What important instruction about corporate worship is found in Hebrews 10:25?

17. On what day did believers in the early church typically get together as the church to worship (1 Corinthians 16:1, 2)?

18. What activities in nature have the potential of enticing men away from corporate worship?

Though Job was impressed with creation, it never became the object of his worship. Instead, creation caused him to worship the greatness of the Creator.

Worship will always be the priority of a godly man.

19. Does creation lead you to worship the Creator, or does it distract you?

Are you using Biblical principles to guide your life in the areas of your source of security and your priority of worship? As a teen, I learned a chorus that summarizes the importance of building our lives around guiding principles centered in God. You might like to use these lyrics as a prayer to start your day.

"With eternity's values in view, Lord,

With eternity's values in view—

May I do each day's work for Jesus,

With eternity's values in view" (Alfred B. Smith).

A Verse to Memorize

> *"But seek ye first the kingdom of God, and his righteousness; and all these things shall be added unto you" (Matthew 6:33).*

A Consistent Man

This lesson will prompt you to practice godliness consistently.

I t's a jungle out there" is a common expression to describe our world. Violence, crude conversation, racial bigotry, and disrespect for people often characterize our society.

Sometimes these practices may characterize a man who calls himself a Christian. He may appear to be pious at church on Sunday, but his words and actions indicate a different character during the rest of the week.

It is easy to fall into the routine of practicing "religion" without evidencing the reality of godliness in our lives.

1. What warning is found in James 2:14–17?

2. What three activities does God desire more than religious ritual (Micah 6:6–8)?

Job was a man who practiced these activities. His life provides a great example of a real man who did not confine his religion to ritual or ceremony but integrated it into his entire life. By demonstrating meekness in his response to enemies, hospitality toward strangers, authenticity in conduct, and respect for others, Job reflected the desires of God.

Meekness

Job was a remarkable example of godly control and graciousness toward others who had been unkind and insensitive toward him. What does it take to press your hot button? Some men have hot tempers. They snap at their critics or enemies and even at their wives. Job refused to respond in that manner— though he did defend his actions.

3. What did Job say he refused to do (Job 31:29, 30)?

4. What did Jesus say was the typical practice when a person was wronged (Matthew 5:38, 43)?

5. What were the names of the men who wrongfully accused Job (Job 4:1; 8:1; 11:1)?

6. What did Job finally do for the three men who wrongfully accused him (Job 42:7–10)?

7. How do you react if someone makes unkind and insensitive comments about you or someone you love?

8. What counsel did Paul share in regard to dealing with people who have hurt you (Romans 12:17–21)?

Meekness requires colossal strength at times. Real men are not only self-controlled; they also act kindly toward those who wrong them.

Hospitality

9. What kindness did Job extend toward strangers (Job 31:32)?

10. What instructions did God give to Israel through Moses concerning strangers (Deuteronomy 24:14–22)?

11. What instruction did Peter share in 1 Peter 4:9?

Getting together with friends is a wonderful experience, but hospitality is more than this. Besides opening his home to family and close acquaintances, Job also entertained many strangers. (The original word for "hospitality" means "the love of strangers.") Job freely gave friends and strangers a place to lodge and food to eat.

12. What are your attitudes, actions, and words toward people who differ in their language, skin color, or nationality?

13. How might you extend kindness to people who appear to be different from you?

Authenticity

Questions regarding the character of top leadership in the United States periodically confront us. The nightly news and morning papers feature stories that prompt us to think about issues such as integrity, honesty, faithfulness, morality, and trustworthiness. Pollsters gather public opinion on the relevancy of character to competency. A significant percentage of the public appears to think that a government official's personal moral decisions are not of primary importance. If a man has the requisite skills and a good track record in job performance, then the character issues do not seem to matter. Many are judging an elected leader's private life by a different standard than his public life.

The potential disparity between our public and private lives has existed since the fall of man in Genesis 3. However, God offers no optional standard for private behavior. He poses one code of conduct regardless of circumstances. In God's eyes, none of life's pressures justify a man's straying from His standards.

14. What did Job imply he had never done (Job 31:33, 34)?

15. How did Adam attempt to hide his sin (Genesis 3:6–8)?

16. What elaborate scheme did David devise to attempt to cover his sin (2 Samuel 11)?

17. What inconsistencies do you detect between your private behavior and your public image?

Respect

Job achieved a high level of business success (Job 1:3). Some men attain that status by taking advantage of people. I have heard a man described as "willing to step on babies and widows" if necessary to achieve his goals. Job acted otherwise; he held others in high regard.

18. What references to disrespect for others did Job cite in chapter 24?

19. What illustrations of disrespect for others have you witnessed?

20. What commitment to ethical business practices did Job acknowledge (Job 31:38, 39)?

21. What consequences was Job willing to accept if he had violated ethical business practices (Job 31:40)?

22. List several ways you might evidence godliness in your business practices.

Are you beginning to see the scope of godliness? A godly character does not come as a prepackaged formula with limited implications. God desires that His character extends through your attitudes and actions to everyone, including enemies, strangers, employees, and customers. Our world needs to see godliness on display.

A Verse to Memorize

> *"He hath shewed thee, O man, what is good; and what doth the Lord require of thee, but to do justly, and to love mercy, and to walk humbly with thy God?" (Micah 6:8).*

Wrap-Up

Real men are godly. Job serves as a dynamic model of determination to live godly in every area of life during both prosperity and tragedy. His example should challenge you to consider the implications of demonstrating God's character in every area of your life.

Write your prayer of commitment to be a godly man.

Answers

LESSON 1

3. God created man in His Own image.

4. Does not seek God; does not do good; is deceitful; has a mouth full of cursing and bitterness; is swift to shed blood; destroys; causes misery; has no peace; does not fear God.

5. All men come short of the glory (character) of God.

6. To be conformed to the image of God's Son.

7. When you confess with your mouth and believe in your heart that God raised the Lord Jesus from the dead, you will be saved.

8. Whatever you do, do everything to the glory of God.

9. Job 3:18, 19—your relationship with your spouse; 3:20, 21—your relationship with your children; 3:22—4:1—your conduct as an employee or as an employer; 4:2–4—your prayer life; 4:5—your witness for Christ and time management; 4:6—your manner of speaking.

10. Perfect; upright; feared God; shunned evil.

11. Cared materially and spiritually for his large family; concerned about many employees; watched over possessions; maintained a testimony for God; cared for the poor, the fatherless, the widows, and the stranger; helped the physically disabled; dispensed justice to those wronged; gave wise counsel as needed.

12. Family—nurture spiritually; Business—manage many employees and possessions; Religious—communion with God; Political—counsel and wisdom to share with the community and its leaders; Community service—care of the poor, fatherless, widows, and those with disabilities.

13. God has given us everything we need for life and godliness.

14. Keep adding to your faith virtue, knowledge, self-control, patience, godliness, brotherly kindness, and love.

LESSON 2

1. Perfect; upright; feared God; shunned evil.

3. All have sinned.

4. Heterosexual (straight), homosexual (not straight); a reference to a lifestyle that adheres to or disregards a moral code.

6. Job acknowledged God can do anything and knows everything. Job recognized that he was a sinner and needed to submit to God.

7. To avoid deliberately.

8. The fear of God causes us to hate evil.

9. Wicked sinners; homosexuality; unrestrained sexual behavior.

11. Young men timidly hid themselves; the aged men stood up; nobles held their peace. They waited for Job's words and listened to what he had to say.

12. A good name is better than riches.

13. Moses—a meek man who kept his power under control; David—a man after God's own heart, ready to do God's will; Judas—a thief who loved money more than God; Demas—a man who loved the world more than God; Diotrephes—a man who loved attention and self more than God and other believers.

LESSON 3

1. Satan.

2. Satan is described as going to and fro, walking back and forth in the earth. The Devil, our adversary, is like a roaring lion, seeking people he can devour.

3. Job feared God.

5. God protected Job and his house, blessed his work, increased his possessions.

6. Let Satan touch everything that Job had.

8. God allowed Satan to touch everything Job had, but Satan could not touch Job.

9. Job 1:13–15—Sabeans took Job's oxen and asses and killed his servants. Verse 16—Fire burned up his sheep and his servants. Verse 17—Chaldeans took his camels and killed his servants. Verses 18, 19—A storm caused his son's house to collapse and killed all Job's children.

10. Job tore his robe, shaved his head, and worshiped God. Job did not sin or charge God foolishly.

11. Job's response did not stop Satan.

12. Job continued to be a perfect and upright man who feared God and shunned evil.

13. Touch Job's bone and flesh, and he will curse God.

14. Allowed Satan to touch Job's body but not take his life.

15. His wife said to curse God and die.

16. He called his wife foolish, saying that they should be willing to receive both good and bad from God. Job did not sin with his lips.

17. Eliphaz—Job has sinned and must suffer. Bildad—Job is suffering because of sin in his life. Zophar—Job's wickedness must be punished.

18. Job was scorned, ridiculed, and treated harshly.

19. Matthew 5:11, 12—Godliness enables us to rejoice and be glad. Matthew 5:43–48—To love, do good, and pray for our enemies. Matthew 10:16–26—To be wise and harmless in conduct and speech; to not be afraid of persecutors. Luke 23:34—To forgive our enemies.

20. To do something well, in clear conscience, and then suffer for it.

21. Christ did not retaliate when insulted and threatened; He committed Himself to God the Father.

LESSON 4

1. Job remembered that God had watched over him and that he had enjoyed an intimate friendship with God. Job's children surrounded him, and he was prosperous and happy. In the city he was honored, and his counsel was respected. Job helped and showed kindness to people in need. Job was a leader whom other men followed.

2. Job was no longer respected. Young rabble-rousers mocked him. No blessings were in sight. He was robbed of the basic enjoyments of life. No one helped him. Job had lost hope regarding the future or of having opportunities to minister to others.

3. (1) Did not look upon a woman; (2) did not practice deceit; (3) did not commit adultery; (4) did not deny justice to his servants; (5) did not neglect people in need; (6) did not trust in his wealth; (7) did not bow down to heavenly bodies; (8) did not rejoice in his enemies' trouble; (9) did not withhold food and lodging to those in need; (10) did not conceal any sin; (11) did not neglect his land.

5. God gave us His Son. He freely gives us all things. God justifies us. Christ intercedes for us, defending us against charges. Nothing can separate us from the love of God. In Him, we are eternally secure.

7. God has promised sufficient grace, one day at a time, to live a life that pleases Him.

LESSON 5

3. A firm adherence to a code of moral or artistic values; honesty.

5. His eyes would not look lustfully at a woman.

6. David let his eyes linger on Bathsheba. He sent for her and committed sexual sin with her.

7. You commit adultery in your heart if you look on a woman with lust.

8. Expect to be ruined and severely punished in this life and judged by the Almighty.

9. The plight of the adulterous man is described as an ox going to the slaughter, a fool to the stocks, an arrow striking the liver, a bird hastening into a snare. He would lose his life.

10. God sees us wherever we are, whatever we are doing.

12. Job did not lie or practice deceit.

13. Job could have overcharged his customers; stolen neighbors' cattle; cheated on wages; refused to keep promises to his employees; labeled meat or hides as higher quality than they actually were.

14. Job was willing to let God evaluate his business ethics.

15. Other people, rather than Job, would benefit from his labor, and his harvest would be destroyed.

16. Unfaithfulness to his wife.

17. He would deserve judgment by God and man, destruction of his reputation, and loss of financial

security for him and his family.

18. Do not go near an adulterous woman; she may look appealing, but she will lead you down the path of Hell. You will lose your honor and wealth. Your flesh and body will be consumed. Follow your father and mother's advice and keep God's commandments. Don't let a whorish woman capture you with her flattering words or by her beauty.

19. Joseph reminded Potiphar's wife of his responsibility to her husband, named the sexual act as a sin against God, refused her sexual advances, and fled the scene of temptation.

21. Deliberately abstain from sexual immorality; keep your body under control to honor God and to be set apart for His use; do not take for sexual purpose that which isn't yours.

LESSON 6

4. Job dealt with employees with compassion and gentleness. Their grievances were settled fairly.

5. Everyone was created by the same God and born the same way.

9. Job 31:6—cared for the poor and for widows; 31:17, 18—fed and reared orphans in his home; 31:19, 20—gave clothing to the poor; 31:21—defended the fatherless.

10. The loss of his arm.

11. Proverbs—If we share generously, we will be blessed; and if we don't share, God will deal with us. Matthew—If we care for the poor and weak, we minister to Christ Himself. Luke—We express our love and obedience to God by showing mercy to needy people whom we encounter. 1 Timothy—A follower of Christ has the responsibility to obey God's command to respect and to provide materially for widows. James—Genuine faith ministers to the fatherless and widows, avoids partiality, provides for the physical needs of believers. 1 John—We evidence our love for Christ by our willingness to sacrifice, even to the point of death, to help those in need.

LESSON 7

1. Our desire to accumulate possessions can become an obsession that consumes our lives. We are in danger of relying on ourselves as the provider of possessions instead of relying on God. Our material goods will not follow us into eternity. We will be bankrupt spiritually.

2. One man's priority is God and his family; the other man's priority is his business to the neglect of his relationship with God and his attention to his family.

3. Job did not stake his confidence in his gold or accumulated wealth.

4. Job recognized that he had come into the world without material goods and would leave the world in the same manner. He acknowledged that God has the right to give and take away possessions.

5. The accumulation of money results in increased temptations and snares. A wealthy individual is more likely to engage in harmful lusts that will lead to destruction. The love of money is the root of all kinds of evil. Greed can cause a person to stray from his faith in God, causing much sorrow.

6. Believers are to be content with the Lord's provisions. By doing so, we will not be seeking to gain more and will be unmoved by external circumstances. God is the source of our contentment.

7. Pursue righteousness, godliness, faith, love, patience, meekness (gentleness). Stand firm in the faith.

8. We need to trust in God, Who gives us all things to enjoy. We should do good works, share generously, be ready to encourage others, and keep an eternal prospective.

10. God abandoned the wicked to pursue their sin. Though men knew God existed, they chose to not glorify God or express thanks to Him. Their thoughts became meaningless, and their hearts became spiritually dark. They viewed themselves as wise, distorting the glory of the incorruptible God into corruptible man and animals.

11. God allows wicked men to follow their own lusts, dishonoring their bodies. They worship idols instead of God and participate in base forms of sexual immorality, such as homosexuality, unrighteousness, fornication, wickedness, covetousness, maliciousness, envy, murder, strife, and other sins. They know they will be judged by God, but they continue to take pleasure in their sin.

12. Job totally rejected idolatry, saying that if he were to worship the creation instead of the Creator, he would be denying God and deserving of God's punishment.

13. Exodus 20:1-6—God commanded that we should not have any other gods before Him and should

not worship any graven images. Psalm 115—God is all powerful; man-made idols of silver and gold are powerless and useless.

14. God is the Creator of the earth, Keeper of the stars and seas, Originator of lightness and darkness, Controller of the weather, Creator of the animal kingdom, and Determiner of the cycles of nature. God contrasted His strength, majesty, and excellency with the lack of those attributes in Job. God contrasted His control of the animal world with Job's inability to order the animal world. God exclaimed that He is indebted to no one; the whole earth is His.

15. Job was speechless; he was humbled. Job admitted his unworthiness. He recognized that God can do everything and that whatever God does is right.

16. We are to assemble together to exhort (encourage) one another.

17. The first day of the week.

LESSON 8

1. We must be careful of saying the right words but not following through with action. Doing good works should be a natural outcome of our faith. We are to demonstrate by our actions what we believe in our minds and hearts.

2. To act justly toward other people, to love mercy, to walk humbly with God.

3. Job refused to rejoice over his enemies' destruction or to use his mouth to curse his enemies.

4. The typical person wants revenge for any wrong done to him.

5. Eliphaz, Bildad, Zophar.

6. Job prayed for the three men as they presented a burnt offering to atone for their sins.

8. Do not do evil to those who have wronged you. Respect those things that are proper and honest. Behave well. Make peace with all men. Commit injustices to the Lord. Care for your enemies' physical needs. Overcome evil with good.

9. Job opened his door and invited strangers to stay at his home.

10. Remember how God took you out of Egypt and redeemed you. Show kindness to strangers, the fatherless, and widows by treating them fairly and allowing them to gather food from your fields, trees, and vineyards.

11. Happily share what you have with other people.

14. Job had no secret sins to hide from God or from the public.

15. Adam sewed fig leaves together for a covering and then tried to hide from God among the trees.

16. David tried to cover up his adultery and Bathsheba's resulting pregnancy by requesting that Uriah, Bathsheba's husband, be sent home from battle so he could have sexual relations with his wife. When Uriah refused to lay with Bathsheba, David requested that Uriah be placed at the front of a battle so Uriah would be killed.

18. The wicked moved boundary lines, stole animals from the poor, and left the poor with nothing to eat, no place to live, and no clothes to wear. They took the children of the poor in exchange for their debts; they forced people to work but did not feed them. They committed murder, adultery, and thievery.

20. Job took care of his land and treated his employees fairly.

21. He would accept weeds and thistles instead of a good harvest.